Unusual Pets

SUGAR GLIDERS

MARYSA STORM

BLACK RABBIT BOOKS

Bolt is published by Black Rabbit Books
P.O. Box 227, Mankato, Minnesota, 56002.
www.blackrabbitbooks.com

BOLT

Alissa Thielges, editor
Rhea Magaro, designer and photo researcher

Library of Congress Cataloging-in-Publication Data
Names: Storm, Marysa, author.
Title: Sugar gliders / by Marysa Storm.
Description: Mankato, MN: Bolt is published by Black Rabbit Books, [2026] | Series: Unusual pets | Includes bibliographical references and index. | Audience: Ages 8-12 | Audience: Grades 4-6
Identi iers: LCCN 2024043370 | ISBN 9781644667828 (library binding) | ISBN 9781644667941 (ebook)
Subjects: LCSH: Sugar gliders—Juvenile literature.
Classi ication: LCC SF459.S83 S76 2026 | DDC 636.92—dc23/eng/20241220
LC record available at https://lccn.loc.gov/2024043370

Image Credits

Alamy Stock Photo/Auscape International, 1, 4–5, 15; Dreamstime/ Ploychan Lompong, 22; Shutterstock/ Africa Studio, 7, AlinaMD, 23, difenbahia, 23, DSlight_photography, cover, EdwinPNursalim, 22–23, Garna Zarina, 22, I Wayan Sumatika, 3, 6, 8-9, 16, 24–25, 27, 32, idea_Photo, 4–5, JessicaGirvan, 23, Kurit afshen, 20–21, Macrovector, 21, Nynke van Holten, 14–15, 28–29, ozkan ulucam, 13, Praisaeng, 26, Prawalapat Nambooppha, 31, Rioji, 13, Salkillust, 10–11, SOMMAI, 18–19

CONTENTS

CHAPTER 1

Meet the SUGAR GLIDER

What a cute, fuzzy animal! It is a sugar glider. It sits on top of a tall shelf. The pet is a long way from the ground. It is not scared though. Neither is its owner. The animal looks around with its big, black eyes. Then, it leaps.

In the wild, gliders eat **nectar**. This comes from fruit.

Sweet Tooth

The animal quickly stretches out its arms and legs. Instead of falling, it sails! It glides right to the coffee table. There, its owner has a bowl of grapes. The little animal takes a piece and chows down. It loves the sweet fruit.

CHAPTER 2

A SPECIAL PET

Sugar gliders are **marsupials**. In the wild, they live in groups called colonies. They are **social** animals. They are most active at night. Wild gliders spend most of their lives in trees. In the dark, they glide from tree to tree. They catch bugs as they go.

WHERE SUGAR GLIDERS LIVE IN THE WILD

NORTH AMERICA

SOUTH AMERICA

EUROPE
ASIA
AFRICA
AUSTRALIA
ANTARCTICA

Bringing One Home

Sugar gliders make sweet pets. They are often curious. They can be cuddly too. People need to check laws before adopting one though. In some places, it is illegal to own one. Lawmakers worry these pets could escape. They might hurt **native** animals or spread diseases.

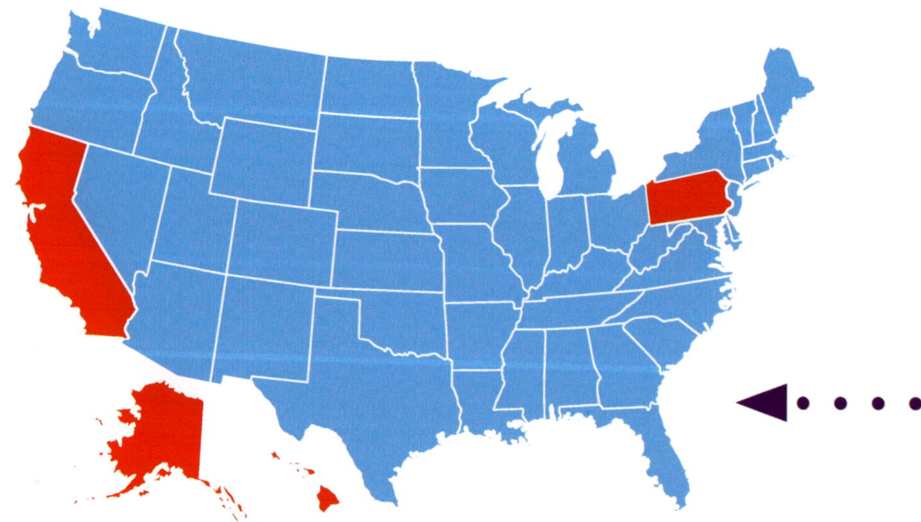

Where It's Illegal to Own a Glider

- Alaska
- California
- Hawaii
- Pennsylvania

CHAPTER 3

Sugar Glider

Sugar gliders have giant, black eyes. They can see well at night. Large ears help them hear well too. Gliders are covered in gray fur. It is super soft and thick. Their bellies are lighter than their backs. A dark stripe runs down their backs.

Average Size

0 1 2 3 4 5 6 7 8 9 10
ounces
ounces
WEIGHT
about
3 to 6
OUNCES
(85 to 170 grams)

Females keep their young in pouches.

How They Glide

Gliders are named after their interesting ability. A flap of skin connects their arms and legs. It stretches from wrist to ankle. When stretched out, the skin catches the air like a parachute. The glider soars. It uses less energy this way. Their long tails help change directions.

PARTS OF A SUGAR GLIDER

LARGE EYES
PINK NOSE

CHAPTER 4

Caring for a SUGAR GLIDER

Caring for sugar gliders can be tough. In fact, a person shouldn't care for just one. These animals are best kept in pairs or groups. Gliders live in large **aviaries**. They need plenty of space to glide. They also need perches to sail to and from.

Gliders need to be kept warm. They like temperatures between 75 to 90 degrees Fahrenheit (24 to 32 degrees Celsius).

A SUGAR GLIDER AVIARY
nest box
with blankets
food
dish
water bottle

toys
bedding

Food and Water

Sugar gliders are **omnivores**. In the wild, they eat a variety of food. As pets, they should be fed **pellets**. For treats, they can have insects, fruits, and vegetables. They need plenty of fresh water too. Gliders should not eat dairy, chocolate, or raisins.

SUGAR GLIDER FOOD

SUGAR GLIDER PELLETS

NECTAR

INSECTS

mealworms, crickets

FRUIT

strawberries, apples, bananas

VEGETABLES

carrots, corn, sweet potatoes

Cuddly Creatures

Sugar gliders can come to love their owners. They will cuddle up with them. Sometimes they even tuck themselves into a shirt pocket. There are difficulties, though. Gliders need to be kept together. They spend the day napping too. Owners say their gentle gliders are worth it, though.

Sugar gliders can't go to just any vet. They need care from vets trained to treat **exotic** animals.

By the
NUMBERS
6 to 8
inches
(15.2 to 20.3 cm)
TAIL LENGTH
15
YEARS
LIFE SPAN

up to
10
NUMBER OF WILD GLIDERS IN A COLONY

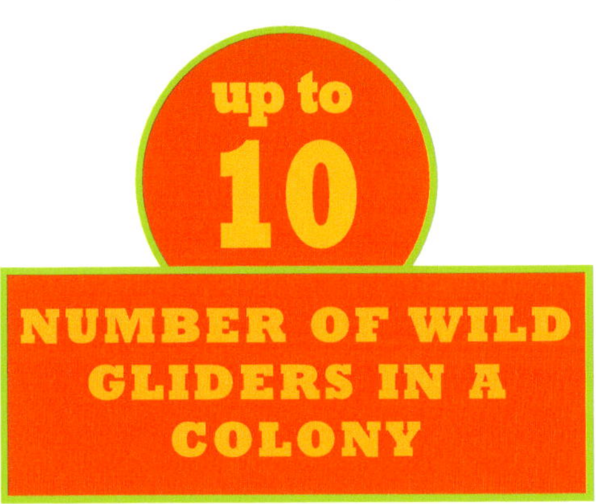

150
feet
(45.7 meters)
ABOUT HOW FAR A SUGAR GLIDER CAN GLIDE

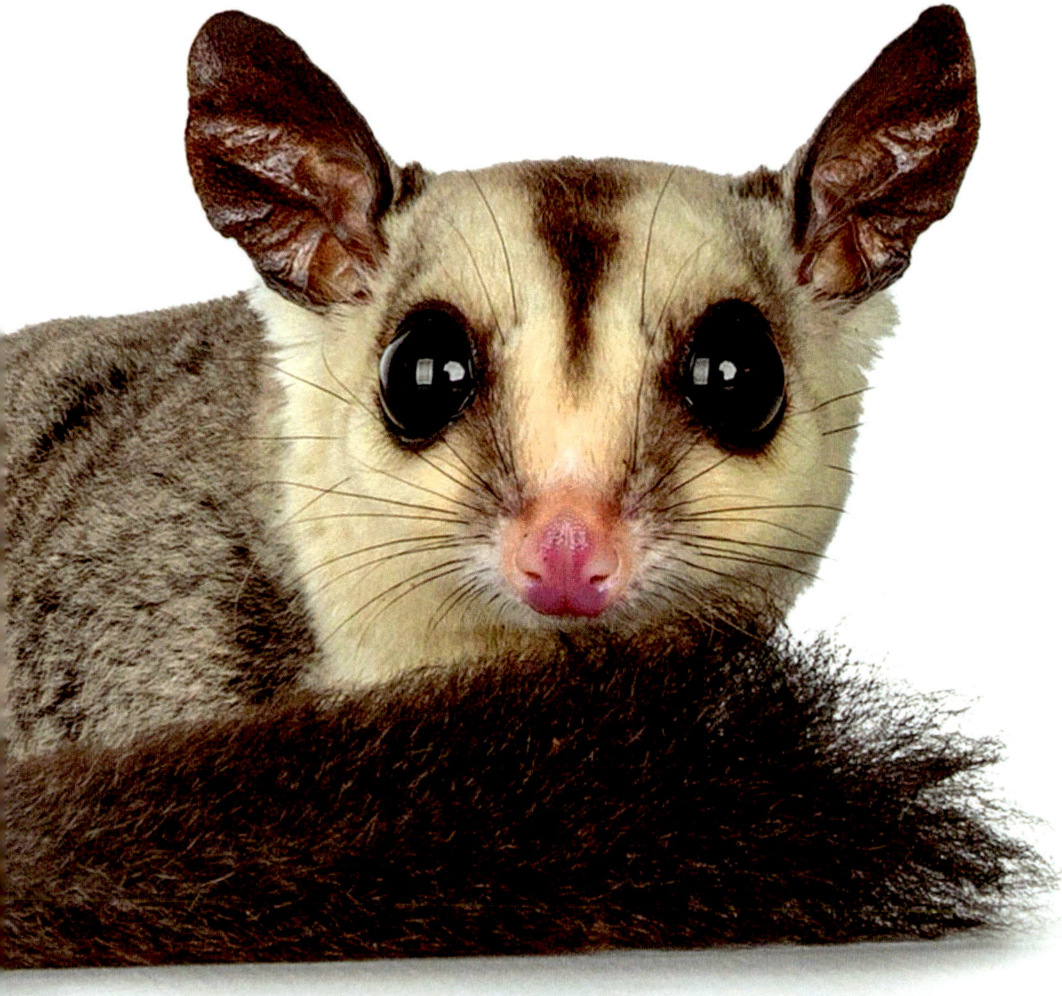

GLOSSARY

aviary (EY-vee-air-ee)—a large bird cage

exotic (ig-ZOT-ik)—from another part of the world

marsupial (mar-SOO-pee-uhl)—a kind of mammal that usually has a pouch on the female to carry young

native (NAY-tiv)—belonging to a particular place

nectar (NEK-tuhr)—a sweet liquid given off by plants and flowers

omnivore (AHM-ni-vor)—an animal that eats both plants and animals

pellet (PEL-it)—a small, hard ball of food

social (SO-shul)—liking to be with and communicate with others

BOOKS

Deniston, Natalie. *Sugar Gliders*. Minneapolis: Jump!, 2025.

Orr, Nicole K. *Awesome Animals of Australia*. Mount Joy, PA: Curious Fox Books, 2024.

WEBSITES

Sugar Glider
animals.sandiegozoo.org/animals/sugar-glider

Sugar Glider Facts for Kids
www.activewild.com/sugar-glider-facts/

INDEX